The
Literary Works
of Me

T0025397

The
Literary Works
of Me

Myrod Byers

TATE PUBLISHING
AND **ENTERPRISES,** LLC

Published by Tate Publishing & Enterprises, LLC
127 E. Trade Center Terrace | Mustang, Oklahoma 73064 USA
1.888.361.9473 | www.tatepublishing.com

Tate Publishing is committed to excellence in the publishing industry. The company reflects the philosophy established by the founders, based on Psalm 68:11,
"The Lord gave the word and great was the company of those who published it."

Book design copyright © 2014 by Tate Publishing, LLC. All rights reserved.
Cover design by Joseph Emnace
Interior design by Mary Jean Archival

Published in the United States of America

ISBN: 978-1-63122-842-1
1. Biography & Autobiography / General
2. Self-Help / Personal Growth / General
14.03.12

Preface

The Literary Works of Me is actually my first body of work, with the exception of college papers, as many of us have written through our journey in life. I have basically put together this book in a matter of three months. I know it was quick. I think what gave me the insight was at one time, I wanted to be a rapper. At an early time in my life, I would talk about many different aspects of life. I would touch on relationships, loyalty, and missing loved ones—whether it be a close family member or close friend. As I would put various sayings on social media sites, I would get a huge response. One day, I woke and said to myself, "Hey, let the whole world see what you have to say." After that, I thought about so many different issues. I then put it on paper.

Growing up, I was always fascinated with Edgar Allan Poe. I believe it's because I had viewed him as a dark person. In my book, I make references to a dark figure, who's sort of menacing, although this is in my dream state more or less. I was also big on Emily Dickinson. I just was tuned into her. It's more of a mystery why. I believe it's because she was so versatile. Her writings applied to all audiences and ages. That is what I am aiming for in my book. I want all groups, ages, and audiences to be able to relate to what I am saying. I cover a variety of different issues, and that is why I titled the book *The Literary Works of Me*. I cover dreams, visions, success, failures, love, and family. These are matters that we all deal with every day. I believe we do it so much, we actually don't think of it in depth. I am hoping to open up the reader's senses to be sensitive to these topics. I want the reader to be just as involved in reading my book as I was in writing it. That is why I did two things with this book. Firstly, none of my sayings are titled. The reason for this is for the reader to connect with what I am saying. Secondly, I numbered my sayings. My thinking was if I numbered my sayings, it would be easier for the reader to reference back to a specific saying. I want all my readers to be able to interact with all that I am saying. Your input is very important to me, as valuable input is always important and a good resource. The ultimate goal is to have every reader feel love and give importance to family values. If you are experiencing hard times, you are not alone.

Welcome to *The Literary Works of Me*. To start, we are going to get into some facts to get the mind moving. So let's go, welcome to my world.

ARPANET (Advanced Research Projects Agency Network)–
   four basic computers that were tied to one another

IP–internet protocol

IBM–first company to make a PC (personal computer)

Earlynet–used transport mechanism

Keyboard–works on a 718-bit system

Bit–1 or 0

Each key on a keyboard is 7 bits

Binary Coding–used for computers

1 = 0–9

2 = 10–99

8-Bit Parallel–bus system

Bus System–is actually on the motherboard

   a. address bus

   b. data bus

Processor–made up of transistors

Processor and Motherboard–have to go together

Chipset–supports the chip; the chipset is what allows the
   processor to work properly

BIOS (basic input/output system)—determines the
   configuration of the computer system

Cold Boot–start-up from the cold position

Warm Boot–start-up from the standby mode

OS–classified as operating system
CPU–central processing unit

    a. It is self- checking
    b. Checks the keyboard
    c. Checks all drives within the computer
    d. Verifies configuration

So how many of you readers knew that? I always thought computers were so interesting. By this point, I am hoping to have the mind grinding.

I prefer not to have titles/names to my sayings. Titles/names leave the owner/author open for critique. Therefore, I will allow the reader to place titles/names to my write-ups. It's all about how you perceive it.

I delve myself in wetness. The wetness consumes me. It takes away my pain. But leaves me feeling depressed afterward. In the end, if I don't overcome the wetness, it will consume me, where death will be evident. Surely, this cannot be my goal.

The heart will only be as heavy and light as the brain allows it to be.

Morning pleasantries, whether they are words or actions, set the tone for how a person's day will begin. Oneself must persevere throughout the day. Sustaining positivity is to be optimistic.

Goals should be set so high, that they are unattainable. If one constantly achieves goals set before them, one becomes complacent. Unmet goals keep one hungry.

Winners do suffer failures. A true winner never succumbs to failure. Their competitive nature will carry them to and across the finish line, whereas a loser is comfortable with just finishing the race. Winners will always find a way to win, by building on their weakness, turning that into a strength.

At times, we think of death at such high frequencies, it actually opens the door for us to the point where we can endure false bravados and courage, enabling us to fall into its hands.

My sole goal is to have my legacy live forever, through my bloodlines and through my work.

You are always destined to be who you wish to be and what you do. And that, my friend, is how you will be remembered.

In life, when you are up, you shall have an abundance of what appears to be friends. In all actuality, all these people are, are "perceptors." What I prefer to call them anyways, because they are there because of your success. They are more likely concerned with human perception. Once your views change, so do your perceived circle of friends.

We often think of gatekeepers in the medieval sense. In all actuality, the gatekeepers of today control every relevant institution that we know to exist—anywhere from education to finance, and everything in between.

This is to bring to light the Christian Crusades and the negative perception of Muslims. In 1095, Muslims effectively ended Christian pilgrimages to the Holy Land. Pope Urban II used the word *infidels* to describe Muslims. The crusaders' battle cry was "God wills it." So are my readers following me. The Muslims' heads were cut off, and they were shot with arrows. To torture the Muslims even longer, the living were tossed into the flames. (This is from *Historia Francorum qui ceperunt Iherusalem* by Raymond D'Aguilers.)

Life is full of ups and downs, full of ins and outs. The goal is to be up more than down and to be in more than out. By that, I mean it's of a strong mind to be more positive than to be negative, to be in your family life, more than you are out of it. Restore family morals and values.

Life is not guaranteed, but death is certain.

I'd rather be situated in a glass house than try to see through a smoke screen.

When you think evil thoughts, the devil lives through your imagination. Your life is motivated by deceit, mistrust, and dishonesty. Therefore you should skip sleeping with the devil. Go to sleep with the maggots, for your homeward descent.

Does medication actually cure/control our illness, or does it give us that boost where we think we feel we are better? As if our sickness was just a mental illusion.

Grinding isn't always about making money. If one states that they are grinding, it should mean that they are moving forward, churning, to move slow but steady. Life in itself is a grind.

Jihad is not a holy war of sorts; instead, jihad is when one is at war with oneself, a person's daily struggle dealing with trials and tribulations.

As I walk through life, I still have not found my calling, as it is not written clearly on the wall. So I keep walking until I come to the correct wall; hell, it might even be a door.

During the night, as I walk through the halls of my residence, the prince of darkness follows me, in a menacing way. He is intently staring at me aggressively. As I walk from the kitchen to the safe room, I wonder if I will make it. Will I become possessed? Why does he pursue me so? Relief as I reach the safe room. I close the door shut. Now I wait for sunrise, when I feel the safest. What are you? What do you want from me? Do I know you? I think not.

One who seeks to live a spacious life is one who wants to rid oneself of extras, of materialistic things that aren't beneficial in one's life. Once this is achieved, one will be able to adhere to their goals and achievements.

Life is in the eye of the beholder in many facets, depending on one's eye for success, achievements, and happiness.

Have you ever wished you could go through life in a retractable bubble? That way, whenever you see bad coming your way, you can always have the bubble to protect you.

When you look up to the sky and see stars, what do you actually see? Do you see promise? Do you see a path to happiness? Do you envision the future and what it holds for you? Or do you see and feel the weight of the world wanting to hurt and crush you?

Have you noticed that pajamas are actually whatever a person has decided to wear to bed that day or night?

Have you ever envisioned walking back in time, wondering what would be your place in that time's society? Would you be a successful person? Would you be a person who experiences many failures? What would be your role in yesterday's society?

One achieves wisdom in a variety of different ways. How much wisdom you wish to achieve is how you go about receiving it.

If you are constantly giving others—whether it be advice, money, or materialistic matters—then who is going to give to you when you are in need? Remember, giving is a free service.

Life is an intangible entity. You can't touch life as a whole or impact it. But a person can always touch and impact another's life.

Today's American culture consists of violence, greed, and money, which are the main ingredients for the recipe of murder.

An energetic person with no foreseeable goals is wasted talent. A person who goes through life fighting battles and achieving small goals is an underachiever. Success in life is not given.

When a person feels gloomy, that is their feeling or vibe. It can last for seconds, minutes, hours, and even days. Sometimes gloom can consume one to the point where they actually make it a part of their everyday life. When one person does this, the gloom begins to harden. Once this is done, depending on the circumstance, the result can be tragic. If you do feel this way, you must uplift yourself to a point where gloom is only a description of the weather.

Reality and life go hand in hand, which makes them interchangeable. At some point, you realize that your life has become a reality. You then realize that reality is actually the very existence in which we live.

If you don't set goals for yourself, then all of your achievements will go unnoticed, especially by yourself. If you don't notice your own achievements, who else will?

When you express a saying as truthful, what exactly are you being truthful about? Yourself, your peers, your family? People that don't matter? Such a saying shouldn't be as such. It should be a self-instilled personal characteristic.

There are plenty of people, things, and situations that can break your spirits. True or false? That would be false! As a spirit has its own intangible characteristic. The only person who is capable of destroying one's spirit is the owner. You have to always be aware of another's negative intentions. Once that is detected, your spirit will stay intact. Because through all the bad, you will still be standing.

When a person states, "In hindsight…," or if they say they have hindsight, do you really realize what they are actually saying? "In hindsight" means to actually be looking back. To say that you *have* hindsight means that you have the ability to look back. "In hindsight" and "having hindsight" are the same. So why do we use the two terms differently?

At times, people say that they are a diverse people or person. But how can you be diverse if your diversity hasn't been tested?

When you wake up in the morning, what is your message for the morning? If you say you haven't been given one, maybe you should lie back down and think about it. Every day, a message is relayed to you. The ultimate decision is whether you decide to acknowledge it as a message.

When we as a country progressed, we began to hinge our success on violence, power, and money. The only way we know how to handle a crisis is by using those three ingredients. The only way to change this way of thinking and life is for us as a country to go back into time and change our way of thinking from the beginning. Then we have to realize, first of all, that this way has been ingrained in us. Secondly, we more than likely will not be the country that we are today. Just food for thought.

Deception is a very deep gene. At times, it becomes so deep, there are people that are deceiving themselves, thinking that they lack confidence to be a better person or to be a more successful individual in life. Sometimes they believe they aren't worthy of life itself.

A person of success is not made, they are born.

If a person states that they have the best laid plan or the element of surprise, the only option is success. You can't have either of these premises and fail.

When you stand before the mirror of life, what do you see? Do you see yourself as the world sees you? Or is it a different reflection? If so, maybe you need to reevaluate where you want to go and be in life.

Your success hinges on your goals laid before you. Your goals hinge on your level of success.

Gratitude is something that is derived from hard work; therefore, we can only be thankful for the things that we have worked hard for.

It's that awkward moment when you are having an interview with multiple applicants, and one applicant is disqualified for failing the drug test. When you hear the news, you look away as if you haven't heard anything.

Success is not gained without trials and tribulations.

At times, we go through life at 100 miles per hour, missing out on the things that are of the most importance to us. Sometimes we have to move like a turtle so we can take everything in when we cross the road of life. On the other hand, we can move like a cat and miss everything important, and may even endure tragedy, because we are trying to cross that road of life without thinking of the repercussions. Or we can choose to move like a turtle—wise, slow, going in a deliberate direction and pace, just to take everything in. Moral of the story: Which roadkill do you see more? Cats or turtles! Exactly.

We all have the option of walking the yellow brick road in our lives. It's the path and desire that we take to get there.

If we choose death over fighting our demons, we will never know if we will be victorious over our strongest enemy, which is ourselves.

A person's life is a map of sorts, where a person goes wrong or gets lost in life itself. It's when they themselves have not created a destination for their life.

In today's society, you always hear people say that they have sacrificed so much for another person. But until you have sacrificed the ultimate, which is sacrificing your own life for the benefit of another life to live, you are just merely doing favors.

I envision a beautiful field full of roses, daffodils, and white and pink lilies. As I walk through the field, careful with every step, the field appears to come to life. I feel refreshed as I walk through this field of newfound life. When I get to the end of the field, I begin to see the bed of roses, daffodils, and the white and pink lilies turn black as death. The grass starts to die, turning a dehydrated brown. Is it me turning things to death? Or am I being pursued by a more sinister entity?

As one's life continues in a downward spiral, the abyss awaits. It's dark and black, and you're unsure if you will come out of the abyss and ride the ship. Or will the verdict for you is to be another tortured soul.

If you have selective listening or even selective learning or even selective criticism, your success in life will be marginal.

The statement "dressed for success" is grossly underrated. In solely listening to the term, it would seem that this would mean a person's outward appearance. Dressing for success must come from within, wherein you're mentally dressed or mentally prepared for all challenges laid before you. Without those things, looking nice will be an epic failure for success.

Tears are the facilitators of the greatest entity of all—emotion. Tears can express sadness, grief, happiness, anger, elation, and sorrow. It all depends on the matter at hand. Hence the statement "Why are you crying?" See, tears aren't so cut-and-dried.

People say they are real or that they keep it 100. When you are these things, you are saying that you are brutally honest, that you will follow the rules/policies/laws regardless of the outcome. In essence, a person who keeps it real or who keeps it 100 will find themselves fired or in the unemployment line; some are in prison, others in the graveyard. There is nothing wrong with being real or keeping it 100, as long as you are aware of the consequences going into that/any situation.

Through the course of your life, there will be people who come along just for the ride. Some of you will be able to dispose of these people at various stops in your life. There is always that person whom you cannot or won't be aware of until the ride is over.

In life, you can lie down and be a failure. Or you can get up and try your hand at success. In my life, I have succeeded a lot, but I have failed even more. But my failures are because I was aiming for success.

It's truly mind-boggling when a person close to you tells you that someone is using you when you offer a helping hand. However, that person close to you is actually the one who has used you a hundredfold. Moral of the story: Before you judge another, you stand in front of the mirror. Now what do you see?

As I sleep, I hear the door creak open. I attempt to open my eyes. But my dream state keeps them locked tight. This dark formidable figure is walking toward me—shapeless, dark, and moves swiftly. Before I can open my eyes, I am swallowed up by darkness.

If you start going through life expecting handouts, at some point, you will need to break this practice. If you stay this way, goals will go unachieved; any achievements will be meaningless to you because you haven't worked for any of them.

If you think about something long enough, you begin to dwell on that topic a little too much. When you begin to dwell on something to a degree, it begins to consume a part of you, making it difficult to overcome.

As I walk in the dark, in the confines of what I call home, I feel as if I am being followed very closely. The hairs on the back of my neck are standing. I begin to walk more briskly toward my safe haven, but my aggressive follower does the same. I finally arrive at my bedroom door. My follower backs away, retreats in the darkness.

Life is like a song within itself. It's composed of highs and lows, of various harmonies. At times, it's smooth and serene. Other times, it can go by so fast that you are unable to grasp what happened or what was even being said. At the end of the day, you have to pick up the genre of life that best fits you and what you can relate to.

It is not when a person dies or how they die, it will be about the impact they leave on the people who are still here on earth and breathing.

When a person values money more than life, the result is everlasting greed, to the point where morals and values become meaningless. A person's success revolves around their morals and values. Without them, at the end, life can become drastic.

At some point in your life, you have to live for a purpose. Only you can know what your purpose in life will be.

When acting on impulse, your thoughts may not be premeditated, but your thought can be the end.

When you list *graduation* as one of the goals that you have accomplished, it is time to set bigger goals for yourself.

Everyone has money in the bank. The mind is rich in thoughts. It just takes willpower to turn those thoughts into action.

When you use people and instances for your own personal gain and/or benefit, in the end, you will be the one to be judged by your own integrity set forth.

To be a successful product of today's society, one must be aware of one's own shortcomings. This can be hard, especially if you are not critical of yourself.

Nothing is fascinating about experiencing the death of a loved one. But it has been known to inspire one to make a lasting impact from that point forward. It has also been known to throw one deeply into the abyss. The key is deciding the balance point between the two.

Society's ways of doing things are in the eyes of the beholder. A person who continues to fail will see it as a hopeless environment. Eventually they will do something to become noticed. The world isn't necessarily a cruel place, but society can be.

As I leave the house and make my way toward my vehicle, I feel the spirits walking in unison with my steps. As I place my key into my door lock, I turn to look behind me. I see a dark cloaked figure, unable to picture or remember its face because there is none. I notice the shotgun as it begins to rise. As I am looking down the barrel of the gun, I think, *Is this my demise?* as there are no words to be exchanged. Is there some evil within me that this figure wishes to rid of, or is there something more sinister at hand?

Common question about death: Is this the end to have a new beginning, or is this the end of it all?

The mind is such a complex and sophisticated organ. If the smartest, most intelligent human being is only capable of using a small portion of the whole, can you imagine where we as a race could be if we could use 50 percent of our mind?

As I see butterflies glide freely through the midmorning air, I often ponder these questions. What does it feel like to have such freedom? Or do these free-spirited creatures actually have freedom?

Only when we actually can feel another's pain, sorrow, and grief can we actually say that we understand another person's pain and grief. Until that happens, we can only say that we are sympathetic to another's mental and emotional state, but not necessarily understanding it.

It is true that knowledge is the key to many doors. But it is all up to the individual to be able to find the right door.

To place one's religion over another or to belittle or believe one religion is superior over another is morally wrong. As God will have it, all are created equally as one. No one or nothing is superior to the Creator.

Has one ever wondered why everything white is of pure content, whereas everything that is black represents darkness or evil? But to mix black and white together brings about gray. In today's world, to enter a gray area is an area of indecisiveness or something that can go either way.

I truly believe that it is a part of human nature to want another's riches, not realizing how hard one has worked to acquire such status or how hard one has had to work to maintain such riches. So to take something of that magnitude from another exemplifies extreme selfishness, which you will be judged and punished accordingly.

One can never see the truth of certain situations if you continue to keep your blinders on.

Associates are meant to come and go through a person's life, as they should, as your goals and achievements change. But if you have friends and family who come and go, then in the end, they were not more than an associate in family's or friend's clothing.

All of us have consciences of different orders; I believe it is okay to listen to your conscience, or even to refer to your conscience, which can be referred to as your gut feeling. The problem comes when you begin to talk to your conscience. That's when your problems begin.

When one has dealt with chaos for the whole of their life, it makes it difficult to deal with a peaceful environment.

When one truly loves a person, it makes it very difficult to let that person go. Even when it is time to let that person go.

Truthfully speaking, nothing is forever. Although at times, we as human beings feel and begin to believe that some things will be forever. When we realize the truth, that's when heartbreak settles in.

When someone says that you have the status of being a lightweight, that person is simply stating that you aren't able to handle stressful situations. Even sometimes, they mean that you aren't as big and tough as they see fit. So at times, mental and physical toughness are characteristics that may need to be proven. Therefore, I don't believe that statement is one that a person should be offended by.

Sometimes a person's intelligence resonates when they use words in an ambiguous way.

When a person walks past a field of souls, I often wonder, do they feel the same as I feel? At times I have a feeling of empathy for all the souls known, also for all the unknown souls.

In order to be a good communicator, a person must be able to reach out to a wide variety of people. It is always good to be able to make people comfortable in the proper setting.

A person's measure of diversity will likely determine their flexibility for success.

A person's insight of love is actually first influenced at birth and the days thereafter. Whether it begins in a positive or negative way, the endearment is likely to affect that person for the rest of their life. No matter how big or small the parent may feel, it will mold that person as they become adults.

Life can be a smooth ride even with waves of turbulence. It is up to the individual to determine if they wish to continue the smooth ride, with minor turbulence, or if they wish for the turbulence to take over. If you decide the smooth path, it is up to you to figure out how and where the turbulence originated. Then you will find out what caused it.

I am not a big believer in the euphoric state of intelligence. I'm not sure if ingesting herbs or the likes of it makes you any more intelligent; rather, it only puts you in a euphoric state of mind. Intelligence is something that is instilled in one's mind over a period, through early-stage learning and instilling discipline for one's desire to learn.

Lots of people not only think within the box, but they also live within that same box. Therefore, they are limiting their own potential in dealing with life skills.

When a parent wishes to be influential in his/her child's life, he/she must develop an adequate level of intuition. A child notices this from within, possibly creating an indestructible bond between parent and child, albeit intuition needs to be applied appropriately.

When you look down at your hands, what do you see? Do you see wear and tear? Do you see youth? When you have the answer, ask yourself, How did they come to this?

When you think back as you get older in life, you should begin to question as to what good deeds you have done in life. Family is not included, as they are an obligation. Hopefully you have done at least ten good deeds. Now think back on how many bad or unrighteous acts you have committed. Now determine the severity of your bad acts/decisions. Which is more resounding? Good or bad? So maybe you have more work to do than you thought.

When you think of what the future holds for you, what do you think/see? Is it clear? Is it cloudy? Is it complete darkness? If it is clear, you as a person know what is expected of you. If it appears cloudy, it is unclear; you *sort of* know where you want to go, you are just unsure of how you are going to get there. If you see complete darkness, basically you don't have a clue what you want to do with life or how you are going to get there.

Believe it or not, a person living in complete darkness has the easiest path, because they have chosen a path where the only way to go is toward the light. They will actually disappoint less people because pretty much nobody has expected anything of them.

What about that moment of anticipation? That moment you are awaiting a word, if you are going to hear the news that you have been waiting for. How many negative thoughts had entered your mind, only to find that you have received good news? Or you were being a person who was so sure of yourself, that you knew you were going to receive good news, when the outcome wasn't as you had hoped? How far did it knock you down? Did you feel you were falsely judged?

About the Author

Myrod L. Byers is originally from Evansville, Indiana. He is from a large family of eight (three brothers and three sisters). His father is from Kentucky, where he was a shoe repairman by trade. He was also an imam. He ran a masjid in Evansville until 1984. Myrod's mother is from Evansville. She worked in the medical field. In 1979, Myrod's family moved to New Harmony, Indiana, where the family bought their first home. This was their residence until Myrod's parents divorced in 1984. Myrod graduated from Evansville Christian School. After graduation, he joined the US Navy for seven years. By 1994, he started a career in the manufacturing industry, where he held various positions through 2013. He got married to Kathleen Lovell in 2006. Myrod's father was very influential in his life as far as instilling family morals and values, which are instilled in his everyday life.

As a child, Myrod was very shy and didn't speak to people he didn't know. He actually didn't come out of his shy state until he went into the military, which was in 1987; at that point, he became somewhat of a comedian. He loves to see other people happy. Upon coming home from the navy, he of course went through trials and tribulations, until he found his place in society. As an early adult, he was very short fused, not sure where this came from, as his parents didn't exhibit that sort of behavior. Myrod prefers to keep his family life very private. His family is his rock; he leans on each one of his siblings for different aspects in his life. It's like each one of them has a specific purpose in his life, which is something he wouldn't trade for anything in the world. Myrod's father passed away from a massive heart attack in 2001, which was the most difficult thing he had endured in his life. He never seemed to think that his father would ever leave, and that's when he experienced the true meaning of a loss. His son Korbin was born nine months after his father passed. Korbin's birth was a great blessing to Myrod. It was a life-changing event. At that time, he began to become more of a cognitive thinker, which allowed him to be a better person. He began to be a person who could actually start to give others advice in dealing with life and what could be done to possibly make themselves better. When dealing with a loss and embracing a creation, everything is looked at differently. Myrod believes that there are some events in life that you shouldn't change for anything.